The Exciting and Social Adventures of Chatting TIMMY!"

Hello, my name is Timmy! Timmy is short for Timothy Bartholomew Harris. I am an only child, which means I don't have brothers or sisters.

This is my bathroom where I wash my face and brush my teeth. My favorite flavor is strawberry and I love to watch it ooze from the tube onto my Thomas the Train toothbrush! My dentist says I should brush for about two minutes, so I hum in my head to the tune of "Ole MacDonald Had a Farm" and I like the cow and duck. That usually gets me to two minutes...

This is my mom- She is the best mom in the whole world! She really understands and supports me because I can be difficult sometimes. I am in the 3rd grade and I go to the Valley Academy. Mr. Canada is my teacher and he is my favorite teacher in the whole wide world! He is cool and all the other kids think he's awesome, too!

My mom always makes a great breakfast for me!

I ride the school bus every day, which means I ride on Monday, Tuesday, Wednesday, Thursday, and Friday. I don't ride on Saturday and Sunday because there's no school, silly.

This is my school bus; it's smaller than a normal school bus. I ride a smaller bus because I don't like large crowds and noise. Sometimes I wear headphones to help me not hear the loud noises. My bus driver usually picks me at 6:37 a.m., which means morning.

This is my school, Valley Academy! I love my school because the teachers really care about me and I kinda like them too...

This is my teacher, Mr. Canada; he is really good with me. He teaches me how to be normal while being myself. Sometimes I feel weird, like I want to cry or pass out and Mr. Canada explained to me that's something called "anxiety." He taught me to take deep breaths and count to ten, whenever I feel that way and when I feel a meltdown about to happen. A meltdown is when I cry, scream, yell, and fall to the floor. Mr. Canada says. "It's not cool to have a meltdown!"

Whenever I get angry or feel like I'm about to have a meltdown, I use the strategies that Mr. Canada taught me. I usually meltdown when my routine is not the same, during math, loud noises, and other things that I don't know of until they happen.

Mr. Canada gets me off the bus every morning and if he is not there, one of the assistants will get me. Also, whenever Mr. Canada is going to be absent, he will tell the class the day before to prepare us. Oh yeah, Mr. Canada's absence causes meltdowns, but I'm getting better at dealing with it.

Every morning, my classmates and I do something that Mr. Canada calls "check yourself", which means we all get together and Mr. Canada says, "Good Morning, friends, I am so happy to be here today! There are five reasons why I'm happy. I'm happy to see Timmy, John, Susie, Thomas, and Lucy." Afterwards, we "check ourselves." By this, we have a chart on the wall that shows pictures of kids showing emotions that range from very happy =1 to angry=5.

I am usually on "happy"=2, but if I'm having a bad morning, I will check myself as "sad".

Whenever any of us checks in as "sad or angry", Mr. Canada will talk to us, individually, about why we are "sad or "angry". Then he gives us a chance to recheck to get at least a "happy". Mr. Canada wants us to begin our day on a happy or kinda happy!

Before we start our day, Mr. Canada gives each of us a "high five!" Usually, I don't really like to be touched, but I am prepared for it, so it doesn't bother me. Mr. Canada says that not wanting to be touched is known as being "tactile defensive." He is so smart!

I went to the playground over the weekend and saw a kid that I wanted to play with… I didn't know how to ask him to play, so I played alone. I told Mr. Canada and he told me he would teach me tomorrow. I can't wait… Well, I need to go to class, but don't forget to join me for my next the exciting, social adventure!